# The Supreme God

This is a work of creative non-fiction. While based on extensive research and rooted in sacred Hindu scriptures, the narrative and characters are fictional. Interpretations of religious texts presented herein are intended for spiritual exploration and are not meant to offend or contradict any individual belief.

**Title:** *The Supreme God*
**Author:** Divyam Agarwal
**ISBN:** 978-93-342-7866-8
**First Edition:** April 2025

Scriptural sources referenced in this book include but are not limited to:
The Vedas, Upanishads, Bhagavad Gita, Mahabharata, Ramayana, Srimad Bhagavatam, Vishnu Purana, and other sacred Hindu texts.

Printed in India

For permissions or inquiries, please contact:
contact@divyamagarwal.com

ॐ

To the One who never leaves,
who protects without asking,
and who lives in the heart of all beings—
this book is for **Vishnu**,
the eternal, the unseen, the Supreme God.

And to every seeker who has ever asked,
*"Who is the real God?"*
May you find Him not in noise, but in stillness.
Not far away, but within yourself.

This is your journey too.

*"Of all that is material and all that is spiritual in this world, know for certain that I am both the origin and the end."*

—Bhagavad Gita, Chapter 10, Verse 39

# Foreword

There are many books about Hinduism, but very few that attempt to ask the question that lives quietly in every seeker's heart: *If there are so many gods, who is the Supreme One?* In a world that often celebrates diversity without understanding its origin, *The Supreme God* dares to search for the singular thread that weaves through every mantra, murti, and myth.

The beauty of this book lies not in doctrine but in discovery. Through the eyes of Eli Walker, a curious soul from another land, we revisit what has always been ours—ancient truths hidden in plain sight. With clarity and compassion, this book walks the reader from temples to texts, from questions to revelations, guiding us gently to the understanding that Vishnu is not one god among many. He is the One behind them all.

This is more than a spiritual book—it is a return to source.

# Preface

The idea for this book was born not out of scholarly ambition, but out of longing. A longing to understand. A longing to unify. A longing to see beyond the symbols and rituals to what they were pointing toward all along.

As I studied Hindu scriptures—Vedas, Upanishads, Puranas, the Bhagavad Gita—I kept encountering the same name, over and over: *Narayana. Vishnu.* Not in small footnotes, but in the heart of the verses. And I began to wonder: How have we missed this?

This book is not meant to convert, argue, or separate. It is meant to connect. To reveal what already exists. Hinduism is vast, colorful, and complex—but at its heart is a simple, loving truth: there is only One, and His name is Vishnu.

Eli's story, though fictional, is deeply human. He is the seeker in all of us—the doubter, the wanderer, the lover of truth. His journey is not just through India, but into the very soul of Sanatan Dharma. By the end, I hope his story becomes yours.

— *Divyam Agarwal*
Author of *The Supreme God*

# Acknowledgments

Writing *The Supreme God* has been a profound journey—one that has been guided by the wisdom of countless teachers, sacred texts, and the inner voice of truth itself. I would like to take a moment to express my deepest gratitude to those who have supported and inspired me throughout this process.

First and foremost, I must thank the ancient scriptures of Sanatan Dharma—the Vedas, Upanishads, Bhagavad Gita, Ramayana, Mahabharata, and the Puranas. Their wisdom is timeless, offering insights into the nature of the Divine, the Self, and the universe. It is through these sacred teachings that this book has found its voice, and I am eternally grateful for the knowledge they have provided.

A heartfelt thank you to the spiritual guides and scholars who have walked with me on this path—those who have helped me interpret the profound teachings of Hinduism with clarity and reverence. Your guidance has been invaluable in helping me navigate the rich, complex landscape of Hindu philosophy and spiritual practices.

To the many saints, mystics, and sages—both past and present—whose lives and words have touched my heart deeply, your examples of devotion, surrender, and wisdom have been a constant source of inspiration. Your lives have shown me that the pursuit of truth is not a solitary endeavor, but a shared journey that connects us all.

A special thanks to my family and friends for their unwavering love, patience, and encouragement. To those who believed in this project from the beginning, your support has meant the world to me. You have been my sounding board, my cheerleaders, and my safe space.

I would also like to express my gratitude to the people of Haridwar, and India as a whole. The sacred land, with its rich cultural heritage, spirituality, and vibrant energy, provided the perfect setting for this story to unfold. It was in the streets, temples, and riverbanks of Haridwar that I found not only the essence of the spiritual quest, but the heart of the truth that runs through all of creation.

To my readers—thank you for embarking on this journey with me. It is my hope that this book will inspire you to ask the same question that Eli did: *Who is the Supreme God?* May your own quest for truth lead you to the realization that the Divine is not far away, but right here, living within you, in every moment.

Finally, I offer my deepest gratitude to Vishnu—the Supreme God, the One who is beyond name and form, who is the essence of all that is. This book is a humble offering to the divine truth that has guided and sustained me throughout my life.

May we all recognize the One who lives in every name, in every form, and in every heart.

With love and gratitude,
Divyam Agarwal

# Table of Contents

# Introduction

If you're holding this book, you may already be wondering about something sacred. Maybe you've asked, like Eli did, "Who is the true God?" Maybe you've stood before countless statues and scriptures, heard the names of many deities, and felt both wonder and confusion.

You're not alone.

Sanatan Dharma—what the world calls Hinduism—is not just a religion. It is a living river of knowledge, experience, and divine insight flowing through thousands of years. It holds truths both mystical and logical, spiritual and scientific. But in its many expressions, sometimes the essence can be hard to find.

This book is a journey to that essence.

Through Eli's eyes, we explore ancient temples, sacred texts, holy rivers, wise saints, and deep inner questions. We challenge the surface idea of "many gods" and discover the truth that was always there: behind every form, there is one eternal source. That source is Vishnu—the Supreme God who preserves all, loves all, and lives in all.

This is not a textbook. It is a story. But every step is based in scripture, every insight drawn from real verses.

It is fiction only in form—its message is as real as the soul within you.

Welcome to *The Supreme God.*

Let the journey begin.

# The Question That Changed Everything

When a disillusioned seeker named Eli Walker arrives in Haridwar from the United States, he's not looking for more stories or symbols—he wants truth. Surrounded by gods, rituals, and unfamiliar devotion, his soul whispers a single question: **Who is the Supreme God?** In the sacred chaos of India's spiritual heart, the real journey begins—not outward, but inward.

---

When a disillusioned seeker named Eli Walker arrives in Haridwar from the United States, he's not looking for more stories or symbols—he wants truth. Surrounded by gods, rituals, and unfamiliar devotion, his soul whispers a single question: *Who is the Supreme God?* In the sacred chaos of India's spiritual heart, the real journey begins—not outward, but inward.

-----

The morning air in Haridwar was soft and smoky, scented with sandalwood, river mist, and the distant breath of incense. Bells chimed in temples. The Ganga River, wide and slow like an ancient whisper, flowed through the city with quiet strength. Pilgrims dressed in all colors moved along the ghats, dipping into the cold water, murmuring prayers, lighting small diyas, and setting them afloat.

Eli Walker stood at the edge of the ghat, shoes in his hand, staring at the river. He had come a long way—from a small coastal town in Oregon, all the way across the world to India. He had left behind his life, his job, his friends. He had even left behind his idea of God.

He had grown up in a Christian home. Church on Sundays, prayers before meals, questions that were quickly silenced. As he got older, those questions grew louder. Why would a loving God allow suffering? Why are there so many religions? Who is right?

College introduced him to philosophy. Life introduced him to pain. His father died of cancer. His marriage ended before it began. He tried meditation, yoga, therapy, silence. Nothing stayed. No answer stuck.

Until he read a single sentence in a book about India: *In Hinduism, God takes many forms but remains One.*

That sentence burned in him. Many forms. One God.

So here he was. In Haridwar. Looking for the One.

-----

His first impression of the city was that it didn't care whether he understood it or not. Haridwar was loud. Full of color. Nothing was in order. People shouted, cows wandered, motorbikes honked. There were shrines on every corner. Statues of gods he didn't know. A blue one with a snake. A monkey-faced one. A smiling woman riding a tiger. Each had flowers, incense, offerings.

He walked past them all, feeling like an outsider. Not just in India. In faith itself.

He stayed at a small guesthouse near the river. The owner, an old man named Suresh, welcomed him warmly.

"You come alone?"

"Yes."

"Good," Suresh said. "Truth is found alone."

Eli didn't know what to say. He just smiled.

Every morning, he sat on the steps of Har Ki Pauri, the main ghat, watching people pray. Some stood in silence. Others cried. Many sang. He tried to understand, but nothing made sense. So many gods. So many ways to pray.

One evening, during the famous Ganga Aarti—when priests light huge lamps and wave them to the river as crowds chant—Eli felt something shift inside him. It wasn't what he saw. It was what he didn't.

In the middle of all that noise and fire and faith, he felt an emptiness in himself.

Not sadness. Not despair.

Just one question.

*Who is the Supreme God?*

-----

That night, he couldn't sleep. The question echoed in his mind. It wasn't about religion anymore. It was about truth. Was there one God behind all these forms? Or were they all real in their own way? And if they were, how could they all be God?

He walked to the river again at midnight. The ghats were quiet. A few sadhus sat under trees, wrapped in orange cloth, lost in meditation. The moonlight made the water look silver.

He sat down and watched the current.

"Looking for something?" a voice asked.

Eli turned. A man in simple white clothes stood beside him. He had no shoes, no bag, no name tag. Just calm eyes.

"I don’t know," Eli said. "Maybe."

The man sat down beside him.

"Sometimes," he said, "we don't look for God. God looks for us."

Eli stared at him.

"Do you believe in God?" he asked.

"I believe in Truth," the man said. "And Truth has many names. But only one face."

Eli didn’t understand. Not fully. But the words stayed.

"How do I find the real God?" he asked.

The man pointed to the river. "The Ganga has many waves, but only one source. If you follow the river long enough, you reach the Himalayas. If you follow truth long enough, you reach Him."

"Him?"

"Yes," the man said. "You will know Him when your heart no longer needs proof."

And just like that, the man stood and walked away.

-----

The next day, Eli went to a local bookstore. He asked for books on Hinduism. The shopkeeper handed him a pile: the Bhagavad Gita, the Upanishads, a few small Puranas translated into English.

He started reading. Slowly. Carefully.

The Gita pulled him in.

*I am the source of all spiritual and material worlds. Everything emanates from Me.*

Who is speaking here? Krishna. A god. A man. A charioteer. But also... something more.

As days passed, Eli kept reading. He visited more temples. Asked more questions.

He spoke with a pandit who told him, "We have many gods, yes. But they are not rivals. They are rays of the same sun."

"Which one is the sun?" Eli asked.

The pandit smiled. "That is for you to discover."

And so Eli began writing a journal. A question journal. Every day, he wrote:

*Who is Vishnu?*

*Why is Krishna called God Himself?*

*Why do some say all gods come from Him?*

*What do the Vedas really say?*

-----

A week turned into two. Eli barely noticed. The chaos of Haridwar no longer bothered him. He was beginning to see patterns. Hidden meanings. Gentle truths behind loud traditions.

One evening, he saw a young girl praying with folded hands in front of a statue of Hanuman. She whispered something, smiled, and ran back to her mother.

"What did she say?" he asked a man nearby.

"She said, 'Thank you for protecting me from fear.'"

Eli looked at the statue. Hanuman, the monkey-god. Fierce, strong, loving.

"Who protects Hanuman?" Eli asked.

"He prays to Lord Ram," the man said.

"And who is Ram?"

"An avatar of Vishnu," the man answered.

There it was again. Vishnu.

That night, Eli opened the Gita again.

*Whenever dharma declines, I descend. To protect the good, to destroy evil, to reestablish righteousness.*

He wrote in his journal: *Maybe the question is not who God is... but what God does.*

-----

On the fifteenth day of his stay, Eli woke up before dawn. The sky was dark. The air cold. He walked to the river and sat quietly.

He had no more plans. No more expectations. Only the question.

The Supreme God.

Not a name. Not a statue. Not a ritual.

But the One behind all of it.

As the sun rose, and light spilled across the river, something in him softened.

Not an answer.

But a beginning.

A stillness.

A voice inside whispered:

*Keep walking. I am waiting.*

Eli smiled.

The journey had begun.

# Many Gods, One Truth

Eli wanders through temples of many deities, stunned by the color, mythology, and reverence that surround each form. But beneath the surface, he senses a thread weaving them all together—a common essence that no one seems to name outright. This chapter unravels the apparent contradiction of many gods in one faith and hints at a hidden unity behind divine diversity.

---

Eli wanders through temples of many deities, stunned by the color, mythology, and reverence that surrounds each form. But beneath the surface, he senses a thread weaving them all together—a common essence that no one seems to name outright. This chapter unravels the apparent contradiction of many gods in one faith, and hints at a hidden unity behind the divine diversity.

-----

The morning after Eli sat at the river in silence, something inside him had changed. The chaos of Haridwar that once felt overwhelming now felt... alive. It no longer shouted at him; it spoke. In symbols, smells, colors, stories. But most of all, it spoke in devotion.

He began his morning with a simple walk through the old town, a notebook in hand. This was his new practice: to observe without judgment, to write without editing, and to ask without fear.

The streets were waking up. Shops were opening, chai stalls bubbling, people sweeping outside their doors. But it was the temples that called to him today. Each one had its own rhythm.

The first he visited was a small shrine dedicated to Durga. The goddess stood tall and fierce, ten-armed, holding weapons and a lotus, a calm smile on her face as she rode a tiger. A priest was lighting a lamp. A woman offered flowers. A child bowed with folded hands.

Eli stood outside the gate, hesitant.

"Come," the priest said with a gentle smile. "She does not reject anyone."

Eli stepped inside. He looked at the statue, the bright red powder, the marigold garlands. It was beautiful. But also foreign.

"What does she do?" Eli asked.

"She destroys evil," the priest said. "And protects her children. She is Shakti—the power behind all creation."

Eli nodded slowly.

"Is she God?"

The priest looked thoughtful. "She is a form of God."

It was the same answer he kept hearing. Everyone was a form. A form of something.

So what was the source?

-----

His next stop was a temple of Shiva. Towering over the street, the white marble idol sat in deep meditation, with ash markings on the forehead, a snake coiled around his neck, and the crescent moon resting in his hair. The air was still inside. Silent. Cool.

A group of young boys came in, chanting "Om Namah Shivaya." Their voices echoed gently.

Eli sat on the floor, letting the chant soak in. The sound was calming. Grounding.

He spoke to one of the boys afterward.

"Why do you pray to Shiva?"

"He gives peace," the boy said. "He is the destroyer of ego."

"Is he God?"

The boy smiled. "He is the Mahadev. The greatest of gods."

Eli wrote in his notebook: *Many gods. Each one greatest. How can they all be God?*

-----

Over the next few days, Eli visited temples of Ganesha, Hanuman, Lakshmi, Saraswati, Kartikeya, and even local village deities. Each one had its own story, flavor, mood. Some were motherly. Some fierce. Some playful. Some wise.

He sat in the temple courtyards. He listened to the priests, the old women, the children. He noticed something: people spoke differently in temples than they did outside. In daily life, they were normal. But in temples, their language changed. It became sacred.

And in every temple, no matter who the deity was, he noticed one more thing:

Somewhere in a corner, small but constant, was a statue or symbol of Vishnu.

-----

"It's like he's quietly watching over everyone," Eli said to Suresh one evening.

The guesthouse owner smiled. "Yes. Vishnu is not loud. He sustains. He holds the world in balance."

"But why so many gods then?"

Suresh sipped his chai. "Different paths for different people. A mother prays to Lakshmi for her home. A student prays to Saraswati for knowledge. A warrior prays to Durga for strength. But the soul... the soul longs for the One."

"And who is that One?" Eli asked.

Suresh didn't answer right away. He looked out at the Ganga.

"Keep looking," he said. "The One is not hidden. He is just silent."

-----

Eli went back to his books. The Bhagavad Gita. The Upanishads. Stories from the Puranas. He began to notice a strange pattern.

In the Gita, Krishna says, *"Those who worship other gods with faith are really worshipping Me, though not in the proper way."*

In the Narayana Upanishad, he read: *"From Narayana were born the Rishis, the gods, and all beings."*

In the Vishnu Purana: *"Vishnu alone is the Supreme Reality. All the worlds exist in Him."

It was like finding pieces of a puzzle.

One evening, he visited a temple that had statues of multiple gods all in one place—Shiva, Durga, Ganesha, Krishna, Ram, Lakshmi, and more. The walls were covered in stories, painted in bright colors. He wandered through the temple slowly.

At the end, he came to a single small room with no statue. Just a flame burning in a lamp.

He asked the priest, "Who is worshipped here?"

The priest smiled. "The One without form. The source of all forms."

"What name do you give Him?"

"We call Him Narayana. The eternal one."

Eli felt a shiver.

-----

He began to dream at night. Not wild dreams, but soft ones. Of rivers flowing into a single ocean. Of stars all turning toward one light. Of temples merging into one grand shrine with no statue, just light.

He started writing less and feeling more.

One day, while watching an old documentary on Hindu philosophy, he heard a quote that stopped him cold:

*"Ekam sat, vipra bahudha vadanti."* — Truth is One, but the wise call it by many names.

It was from the Rig Veda.

He looked it up in his book.

Yes, it was there.

The oldest book of all.

The Vedas themselves had said it from the beginning.

Eli stood up. He felt light. Like a weight had shifted.

He still didn't have the full answer.

But he had a glimpse.

Not all gods were separate.

They were mirrors.

Reflections.

Guides.

And maybe, just maybe, they were all pointing to the same place.

To the One.

To Vishnu.

-----

At night, he returned to the river. The moon was high. The water glowed.

He closed his eyes and whispered:

"If You are One, show me the way. I will follow."

A breeze touched his face. The river moved gently.

And in the stillness of the night, Eli felt it again.

Not noise.

Not confusion.

But a presence.

Not many.

One.

And the journey continued.

# The Oldest Books Speak

Led by curiosity and sacred chance, Eli is introduced to the Vedas—Hinduism's oldest and most authoritative scriptures. To his surprise, they don't describe hundreds of gods, but instead declare one eternal Being: Narayana. As he explores ancient mantras and forgotten verses, Eli begins to see that the truth was never hidden—it was always in plain sight.

---

Eli's time in Haridwar had become a dance between questions and answers, between doubts and glimmers of insight. The more he learned, the more he realized that the questions weren't just about finding the answers—they were about understanding a truth that had always been there, hiding in plain sight.

After weeks of wandering, visiting temples, talking to priests, and scribbling notes in his little journal, Eli knew something deep within him had shifted. The question that had burned in his heart—Who is the Supreme God?—was still alive. But now, something else stirred beneath it: a new question. *If Vishnu is the One, where do I find Him?*

One evening, after a long day of temple-hopping, he sat down with Suresh. The two of them often shared chai and exchanged thoughts about Eli's journey. Tonight, Eli felt a burning curiosity.

"I've seen a lot of gods," Eli began, his voice still soft with awe. "But I keep hearing about Narayana. Who is he?"

Suresh took a sip from his cup, eyes thoughtful. "Narayana is another name for Vishnu. He is the One who pervades all things. He is the Source."

Eli frowned, trying to put the pieces together. "But I thought Vishnu was just one of the gods. How is He the Source?"

Suresh smiled warmly, his eyes gleaming in the soft light. "That's the journey you're on, Eli. To understand how the One appears as many. Narayana is not hidden; He is simply not always recognized."

Eli felt a small weight lift from his shoulders. "I think I need to understand more... about the scriptures. The Vedas."

Suresh's eyes sparkled. "Ah, you're ready. The Vedas will answer your questions. But they might not give you answers like you expect."

-----

That night, Eli took out his book on Hindu philosophy, a text given to him by one of the local scholars. It was dense, filled with words that were foreign and confusing. But there was something about the way the words felt in his hands, something sacred. He turned the pages slowly, soaking in the ancient script, until a word caught his eye: *Narayana.*

It was mentioned briefly in one of the Upanishads. The text described Narayana as the "Supreme Being," "the one from whom all things emanate." Eli's heart quickened. There it was again—the idea that all gods, all stories, all paths, eventually lead back to this one eternal presence.

He read on. The more he studied, the more he realized that the Vedas didn't describe a pantheon of gods in the way he'd imagined. They spoke of a singular, all-encompassing force, beyond names, beyond forms. It was the One behind the many—the ultimate reality that no single image could capture.

-----

The next day, Eli decided to seek out someone who could explain these ideas more clearly. He went to meet with a scholar, a learned man named Swami Haridas, who lived in a quiet ashram on the outskirts of the town. Eli had heard whispers that Swami Haridas was an expert in the Vedas, so he hoped that perhaps the answers he sought might lie in the swami's words.

Swami Haridas greeted him warmly. His hair was long and silver, his eyes deep and wise, like someone who had seen the world in its many forms and still found peace in the stillness beneath it all.

Eli explained his journey, the questions that had been arising, the tension between the many gods he'd encountered, and the understanding that something deeper, something more fundamental, was emerging. He told the swami about the mention of Narayana and Vishnu and his desire to understand more.

Swami Haridas listened carefully, nodding in approval. "You are on the right path, Eli. The Vedas speak clearly—if you have the ears to hear."

Eli was eager. "Tell me, swamiji, how do I begin?"

The swami smiled, his eyes twinkling. "We begin with the oldest words, the words that came first. In the Rig Veda, the first of all the Vedas, we hear a voice that says, *Ekam sat, vipra bahudha vadanti.*" He paused for a moment, allowing the words to sink in.

Eli frowned. "What does that mean?"

Swami Haridas closed his eyes briefly, then spoke. "It means, 'Truth is one, but the wise call it by many names.' This is the heart of what the Vedas teach. They tell us that all paths, all gods, all names are merely different reflections of the One truth, which is Narayana—Vishnu."

Eli sat back, taking in the weight of the words. *Truth is one.*

He felt the sensation of something vast, something ancient, stirring within him. This was it. This was the key.

-----

The swami continued. "In the Vishnu Purana, it is said that Vishnu alone is the Supreme Reality. He is the cause of the creation, the sustainer of life, and the ultimate dissolution. All worlds exist in Him, and from Him, they are born."

Eli pulled out his notebook and scribbled down the words. He had been right. The many gods, the hundreds of names, the vastness of it all—it all pointed to the same truth.

"But why don't people see it?" Eli asked. "Why is it so hidden?"

Swami Haridas smiled gently. “Because the truth is not a thing you can touch with your hands or see with your eyes. It is something you must feel in your heart. The gods are not false. They are real, but they are only reflections of the One. Like mirrors showing different aspects of the same face.”

Eli nodded slowly, understanding dawning on him. “So, the gods... they’re not separate. They’re all part of the same truth?”

Swami Haridas nodded again. “Exactly. In the Upanishads, we learn that Narayana is the cause of all things. Everything in the universe—from the smallest atom to the largest star—exists within Him. He is the soul of everything.”

Eli’s mind raced. The answers were starting to connect. The Vedas, which he had once seen as a collection of myths and rituals, were actually a guide to understanding the ultimate truth—the One God. Not just any god, but Vishnu, the sustainer, the protector, the eternal.

-----

As he left Swami Haridas’s ashram that afternoon, Eli felt like the pieces of a puzzle were slowly coming together. He walked along the Ganga, his thoughts swirling with new ideas. The river flowed beside him, a quiet, constant reminder of the divine flow that connected all things.

He returned to his guesthouse and opened his book on the Vedas again. He read passages from the Rig Veda, the Sama Veda, and the Yajur Veda. Each verse seemed to weave a story about Vishnu's eternal nature, about how He pervaded all of existence.

In the Upanishads, he read these words: *"From Narayana were born the Rishis, the gods, and all beings. He is the beginning, the middle, and the end of everything."* The truth felt clearer now—Vishnu was not a part of God. He was God, the One who held all things together.

-----

That night, Eli's dreams were vivid. He saw rivers flowing into the ocean, stars swirling around a central light, temples of all forms merging into one—a grand, eternal temple with no idol, no image, just pure light. It was as if the universe itself was telling him, showing him the truth.

He awoke the next morning, feeling different. The question that had haunted him for so long was still there, but now he felt less desperate to answer it. He had caught a glimpse of something profound, something eternal.

Eli looked out over the Ganga, his mind quiet but full. The journey was far from over, but now, at least, he knew that the truth was not hidden. It had always been in front of him—just waiting to be recognized.

-----

In the days that followed, Eli continued to study the Vedas, the Upanishads, and the Puranas. The scriptures were clear. Vishnu was the One. He was the source of all creation, the sustainer of all life, the destroyer of all that was unnecessary, and the eternal force that held the universe in balance. Every god, every deity, every path, was a manifestation of the same truth.

He returned to Suresh one evening, the sun setting behind the mountains.

"You were right," Eli said with a smile. "I've been looking at it all wrong. It's not about many gods. It's about one truth, and all the gods point to Him."

Suresh nodded, his face full of knowing. "Yes, Eli. The One is always with you. In the light, in the darkness, in every name, in every form."

Eli closed his eyes, breathing in the stillness of the evening. The river's gentle flow reminded him of the eternal presence of Vishnu. And with that realization, his journey continued.

# The One Who Never Takes But Always Preserves

Among the trinity of Hinduism, one figure stands apart—not demanding worship or sacrifice, but offering preservation and peace. As Eli studies the role of Vishnu through history and mythology, he finds a divine pattern of love, balance, and protection. In a world full of chaos, Vishnu is the one who holds it all together.

---

The Ganga was as tranquil as Eli had ever seen it, flowing with a quiet, steady rhythm that reflected the peaceful feeling growing within him. The lessons of the Vedas, the Upanishads, and the Puranas were settling in his heart, but Eli knew he wasn't done yet. His mind still wrestled with the complex mystery of Vishnu. He'd learned that Vishnu was the One—the Source, the Eternal, the Supreme God behind everything—but the more he studied, the more he realized there was still so much to understand.

The question that lingered in his mind was: *What role does Vishnu play in all of this?* He knew Vishnu was not like the other gods, demanding sacrifice or praise. Vishnu didn't need anything from humanity. He wasn't a god who needed to be appeased, like so many others in the pantheon of deities. Instead, he was the preserver, the protector, the one who held everything together.

Eli was sitting by the Ganga one afternoon, reflecting on his journey. His mind wandered back to the many gods he had seen in Haridwar—the countless idols, each with their own myth, their own story. Some of the gods, like Shiva, were intense and wild, embodying the destruction that was necessary for rebirth. Others, like Lakshmi, were symbols of wealth and fortune, guiding the faithful toward prosperity.

But Vishnu was different.

He wasn't a god who demanded to be worshipped with elaborate rituals. He wasn't a god who needed to be feared. Vishnu, Eli realized, was the one who quietly watched over creation, ensuring its balance, its flow. He wasn't just a god of the past—he was a living presence, always there, sustaining and protecting. And yet, unlike the others, he never took. He only gave.

-----

The next day, Eli visited Suresh once more, eager to explore his thoughts about Vishnu's role. As they sat together, drinking chai, Eli spoke of the realization that had settled in his heart.

"Vishnu doesn't take anything from us, does He?" Eli asked, his voice thoughtful. "He doesn't demand worship or sacrifice. He just preserves."

Suresh smiled, nodding. "Exactly. Vishnu's role is unique. He is the sustainer of all life. He preserves the universe, making sure that the balance is maintained. In every age, in every yuga, Vishnu's primary task is not to create or destroy, but to protect. He keeps the order of the cosmos intact, like the steady hand of a gardener who nurtures the plants, but doesn't take credit for their growth."

Eli's brow furrowed in curiosity. "But how does he do that? How does he preserve everything?"

Suresh leaned back, his eyes thoughtful. "Let's look at it this way: In every yuga, in every era of time, the universe goes through cycles of creation, preservation, and dissolution. Vishnu's role is always the same: to preserve. He doesn't interfere unnecessarily, but he ensures that the world remains balanced."

-----

Eli listened carefully, his mind racing with ideas. "I've been thinking a lot about Vishnu's avatars," he said. "Each one seems to appear when the world is in chaos, when balance is lost. It's like he's always there, stepping in when things get out of control."

Suresh nodded. "Yes. Vishnu's avatars—whether it's Krishna, Rama, or Narasimha—are not just stories. They are the actions of the divine to restore balance. When the world is in turmoil, when dharma is threatened, Vishnu manifests in a form that is most needed. But He doesn't seek glory or praise. He comes to protect and restore."

-----

As Suresh spoke, Eli's thoughts drifted to the stories he had read in the Bhagavad Gita and the Ramayana. In both, he saw a recurring theme: Vishnu's avatars always came when humanity was in desperate need of protection. He remembered the story of Rama, who fought to rescue Sita from Ravana, not for his own glory, but to restore dharma, the cosmic law.

Vishnu, as Rama, had not asked for anything. He had only given—his strength, his courage, his devotion to dharma.

And then there was Krishna, the playful, charming figure who appeared in the Mahabharata. Krishna, too, didn't demand anything from Arjuna. He didn't force Arjuna to fight in the great war. Instead, He offered wisdom, guidance, and protection. Krishna's role was to restore balance between good and evil, not by taking anything, but by ensuring the right path was followed.

-----

Eli looked up at Suresh. "So, Vishnu's avatars are like... acts of love?"

Suresh smiled softly. "Yes. Vishnu's avatars are acts of love for humanity. He doesn't come to take control. He comes to preserve what is good, to protect what is just, and to guide the lost back to the right path. Every time He manifests, it is because the world is teetering on the edge of chaos, and He steps in to restore harmony."

Eli felt a warmth spread through his chest. "That's beautiful," he said quietly.

-----

As the days passed, Eli's understanding of Vishnu deepened. He spent hours reading more about the avatars—each one revealing a new aspect of divine love and protection. He read about Vishnu's first avatar, Matsya, the fish who saved the ancient scriptures from the great flood. He learned about Kurma, the tortoise, who supported the mountain used to churn the ocean of milk. And he was fascinated by the story of Narasimha, the man-lion, who protected his devotee Prahlada from the evil king Hiranyakashipu.

Each story told of Vishnu's unwavering commitment to the preservation of life, justice, and dharma. But what struck Eli the most was how Vishnu never asked for anything in return. Unlike the gods who demanded rituals, offerings, and sacrifices, Vishnu was the one who gave and gave without expectation.

-----

One evening, as Eli sat by the river, he began to see the bigger picture. The universe, he realized, was a delicate balance—a balance that Vishnu held in place. Life and death, creation and destruction, were all part of the same cycle. Vishnu, as the preserver, didn't control or manipulate. He allowed life to flow naturally, ensuring that it never tipped too far into chaos.

In that moment, Eli understood something profound. The reason Vishnu didn't demand worship was that His presence was already a gift. Life itself was His offering, His preservation of the universe. By simply existing, He provided the balance the world needed.

-----

Eli spent the next few weeks meditating on these ideas, reflecting on Vishnu's role as the one who preserves. He meditated in the temples, where the sounds of bells and chants filled the air, and he felt a deep sense of peace in his heart. He visited the ghats of the Ganga, watching as people came to offer prayers and immerse themselves in the holy waters. But for Eli, it wasn't the rituals or the offerings that mattered anymore. It was the understanding that Vishnu was always present—preserving, protecting, loving.

One evening, while walking along the river, Eli encountered an elderly man who had been sitting in silence by the water. His face was peaceful, his eyes wise with age. Eli approached him, feeling drawn to the stillness the man radiated.

The elderly man smiled warmly. "You are a seeker, I can tell. What is it that you seek, young one?"

Eli sat down beside him. "I've been searching for the truth. I've been asking, *Who is the Supreme God?* And I think I've found Him."

The elderly man nodded slowly. "Ah, Vishnu. The Preserver. The One who holds all things together."

Eli felt a warmth in his chest. "Yes. I've learned that Vishnu doesn't take from us. He only gives. He's the one who preserves everything—life, love, balance."

The old man's eyes twinkled. "You are learning well. Remember this: To truly understand Vishnu, you must learn not to take, but to give. He is the source of all preservation, and true peace comes when we stop asking for more and begin offering what we have."

Eli sat quietly, letting the old man's words sink in. As the Ganga flowed beside them, Eli realized that Vishnu's presence was more than just a belief. It was the flow of life itself—the quiet, steady force that held everything in place.

-----

As Eli continued his journey, he felt a deep sense of gratitude. He had found something powerful within himself—a peace that came from understanding that the One he sought was not distant or demanding. Vishnu, the Preserver, was always with him, always offering balance, always offering love. And it was in this understanding that Eli found the beginning of his own peace.

# Shiva, Devi, and the Illusion of Separation

Are Shiva, Devi, and Vishnu rivals—or reflections of the same truth? This chapter takes Eli into the heart of spiritual philosophy, where saints and scriptures reveal the non-duality hidden beneath every form. What appears as separation is unity playing dress-up. God, it turns out, wears many faces—but speaks with one voice.

---

Eli's journey had taken him deep into the heart of India, and in that quiet space of his soul, a truth was beginning to take shape. He had seen Vishnu's presence everywhere, in every verse and every temple. Yet, as he wandered further, Eli began to feel a tension, an unease that something was missing in his understanding. Was Vishnu the only god? Was there something more to this intricate dance of divine deities? Was Vishnu really the Supreme God, or were there other gods competing for that title? Questions like these lingered in Eli's mind as he walked beside the Ganga, feeling the weight of the mysteries he had yet to uncover.

One evening, as the sun began to set, painting the sky with hues of orange and pink, Eli sat on the ghats, watching the river's endless flow. It was then that he noticed a group of devotees gathered around a small shrine, chanting mantras and offering flowers. The idol was that of Shiva, the great god of destruction, sitting in his meditative pose, his third eye half-closed. Eli watched them for a while, fascinated by the intense reverence these people had for Shiva.

But something about it stirred a question in his heart: *If Vishnu is the Supreme God, then what is the place of Shiva?* Were they rivals, as some believed? Was there a deeper connection between them? And where did the goddess Devi fit into all of this?

Eli's thoughts drifted back to the teachings he had received from Suresh. He remembered how Suresh had told him that Vishnu was the Preserver, the one who protected life and maintained order. But what about Shiva, the destroyer? And what about Devi, the goddess who represented Shakti, the divine feminine energy? Were they separate, distinct beings, or was there something more?

-----

The next day, Eli sought out Suresh again, hoping to find some clarity. As always, they sat together in the small, quiet temple by the Ganga, where the sounds of the river mingled with the gentle whispers of the wind. Eli spoke with urgency.

"Suresh, I've been thinking," Eli began. "If Vishnu is the Supreme God, then where does that leave Shiva and Devi? Are they different gods, or are they part of Vishnu' s essence?"

Suresh smiled, his eyes filled with warmth. "Ah, Eli, you are asking the right questions. Let's begin with this: In Sanatan Dharma, there is no true separation between the gods. What you see as different faces of God are actually reflections of the same eternal truth. Shiva, Vishnu, Devi—they are all manifestations of the same divine essence, each playing a unique role in the great cosmic drama."

Eli furrowed his brow. "But Shiva and Vishnu are often shown as opposites. Shiva is the destroyer, and Vishnu is the preserver. How can they be the same?"

Suresh leaned forward, his voice calm and steady. "Shiva is not the opposite of Vishnu, Eli. He is a part of the same divine unity. Destruction, in the Hindu view, is not something negative. It is a necessary part of the cycle of creation. Without destruction, there cannot be creation. Without the destruction of the old, the new cannot be born."

-----

Suresh continued, explaining how the universe moves in cycles of creation, preservation, and destruction. Vishnu, the preserver, ensured that the universe maintained balance, while Shiva, the destroyer, cleared away what was no longer needed. The destruction Shiva brought was not about annihilation, but about making space for new life, new possibilities.

Eli's mind began to unravel the complexity of this idea. Destruction was part of creation, just as night was part of day. Without one, the other could not exist. Shiva's role wasn't to fight Vishnu, but to complement him. Together, they formed a dynamic partnership in the eternal dance of the universe.

"But what about Devi?" Eli asked, his curiosity piqued. "Where does she fit into all of this?"

Suresh's smile deepened. "Devi, or Shakti, is the divine feminine energy. She is the power that drives everything in the universe. Without Shakti, there would be no movement, no action. Vishnu, Shiva, Brahma—all of the gods depend on Shakti for their power. In a sense, Devi is the source of their strength, the energy that brings everything to life."

Eli took a deep breath, trying to absorb all of this. He could see now that what appeared to be separate deities—Shiva, Vishnu, Devi—were actually different expressions of the same ultimate truth. Each had its own unique role, but they were all connected, all part of the same divine unity.

-----

In the following days, Eli visited temples dedicated to each of these gods. He wandered through shrines to Shiva, admiring the intricate carvings of his cosmic dance, his third eye, and his fierce determination. He sat in the presence of Vishnu, feeling the deep calm that radiated from his images of peace and balance. And he visited temples of Devi, where the air seemed alive with the powerful energy of the goddess, the source of creation and destruction.

Everywhere Eli went, he felt a sense of unity—unity not in spite of their differences, but because of them. Shiva, Vishnu, and Devi were not competing for supremacy. They were parts of a grand, divine harmony, each one necessary for the universe to function.

But there was still a lingering question in Eli's mind: *How could so many people believe in these gods as separate?* If they were all part of the same divine essence, why did it seem like they were worshipped in isolation, each with its own following and rituals?

Eli's answer came one afternoon when he met a wise old woman sitting by the Ganga. She was dressed in simple clothes, her hair tied back in a loose bun. Eli sat beside her, sensing that she carried deep knowledge.

"You look troubled, young man," she said with a kind smile.

"I am," Eli replied. "I've been learning so much about the gods of Hinduism, and yet I still feel like I don't fully understand. I know Vishnu, Shiva, and Devi are all part of the same divine essence, but why do they appear so separate?"

The old woman nodded gently. "Ah, this is the illusion we all face. The illusion of separation. You see, the divine truth is one, but when it enters the world of forms, it takes on many faces. The gods are not separate from each other, but their forms help us understand different aspects of the one truth. Each face of God speaks to a different part of our soul."

Eli felt a sudden clarity. "So, the gods are different faces of the same truth, each one pointing to the same ultimate reality?"

The old woman's eyes sparkled. "Exactly. Just as you see different reflections of the moon in the water, each reflection appears separate, but they are all the same moon. Similarly, the gods may seem separate, but they are all reflections of the same divine essence."

Eli's heart swelled with gratitude. He felt the pieces of the puzzle finally coming together. The illusion of separation was just that—an illusion. The gods were not rivals; they were reflections of the same truth, wearing different costumes to help humanity understand the many aspects of the divine.

-----

As Eli continued his journey, he realized that the gods were not fighting for supremacy. Vishnu, Shiva, and Devi were not rivals—they were different expressions of the same eternal truth, each one necessary for the harmony of the universe. Each face of the divine spoke with a different voice, but all of them were pointing to the same reality.

And in this understanding, Eli found peace. He no longer saw the gods as separate, but as one divine force, manifesting in different ways to guide humanity. He had learned that true wisdom came not from seeing the differences between the gods, but from seeing the unity that lay behind them.

In this realization, Eli felt a deep sense of connection to the universe and to the divine. He understood now that the divine was not something to be feared or understood in fragments—it was something to be experienced in its fullness, in all its many forms. And in that fullness, he found the true heart of God.

# The Avatars Are Not Just Stories

Ram. Krishna. Narasimha. Vamana. These are not just ancient tales to Eli anymore—they are living echoes of a divine presence that descends whenever the world forgets its source. As Eli journeys through these stories, he begins to see them not as legends, but as love letters from the Divine, each one saying: **I have not left you.**

---

The more Eli traveled through India, the more his understanding of the divine deepened. The mystery of Vishnu, Shiva, and Devi had begun to unravel, and yet, something still tugged at his heart. It was the idea of the avatars—those divine manifestations that appeared on Earth whenever the balance of the world was threatened. Ram, Krishna, Narasimha, Vamana—the names were familiar, even to him, a foreigner from the United States. But they had always seemed like distant myths, mere stories to explain the world's chaos.

Now, they seemed something more.

As Eli walked through the winding streets of Haridwar, he thought about the teachings he had received. He had learned that the gods were not separate from each other, but expressions of the same divine truth. He had understood that Vishnu, the Preserver, was the one who held the universe together. But these avatars—these incarnations of the divine—were still a mystery. What did they mean? Why had they appeared, and what did they have to do with him, with his search for the Supreme God?

It was during one of his early morning visits to the Ganga River that Eli first heard the term "avatar" in a new light. He had been sitting by the river, watching the sunrise, when a group of pilgrims approached. They were chanting softly, their faces filled with devotion, as they made their way to the water to bathe and offer prayers. Among them was a man, older than the rest, with a peaceful expression. Eli, always eager to learn, approached him with a respectful bow.

"Excuse me, sir," Eli began, "can you tell me about the avatars of Vishnu?"

The man turned to him, his eyes bright and wise, as though he had been waiting for this very question. "Ah," he said, "the avatars are not just stories, my friend. They are living truths, manifestations of the divine that come to remind us of who we are, and of the love that binds us all."

"Living truths?" Eli repeated, puzzled. "But I've always thought of them as legends—stories from the past."

The man smiled gently. "Many people do. But the avatars are more than stories. They are not bound by time. They come whenever the world forgets its source, whenever humanity falls into darkness. And they are not just from the past. The divine does not leave us—it is always here, always watching over us, guiding us."

-----

Eli felt a stir in his heart, a deep sense of wonder. The idea that the avatars were not just ancient stories, but living reminders of the divine presence, made sense to him. These incarnations of Vishnu were not distant events, but ongoing expressions of divine love.

"Tell me more about the avatars," Eli said, his curiosity growing.

The man nodded and began to speak, his voice calm and steady, like the flowing river. "The first avatar was that of Matsya, the fish. In the ancient times, the world was flooded, and the sacred knowledge of the Vedas was about to be lost. Vishnu, in the form of a fish, saved the holy scriptures and brought them safely to the sages."

Eli listened intently, but it was the next avatar that truly captured his imagination: "The second avatar, Kurma, the tortoise, was when Vishnu took the form of a great tortoise to help the gods churn the ocean of milk to obtain the nectar of immortality. This story is not just a tale of struggle, but of cooperation—gods and demons working together for a common goal."

Eli's mind began to connect the dots. Each avatar wasn't just a random story—it had meaning, a deeper significance. Vishnu, in his divine wisdom, came in different forms to restore balance to the world. These avatars were not just mythological figures—they were divine actions, divinely timed.

The man continued: "The third avatar, Varaha, the boar, saved the Earth from the demon who had taken it into the depths of the ocean. Vishnu, as the boar, plunged into the waters, lifted the Earth, and restored balance."

Eli's heart beat faster. He could see the divine pattern now. Vishnu wasn't just protecting the world from destruction—he was reminding humanity of the eternal truth, restoring balance not just to the Earth, but to the human soul.

"The fourth avatar," the man continued, "is Narasimha, the half-man, half-lion. Vishnu took this form to protect his devotee Prahlada from his evil father, Hiranyakashipu. The demon king had declared himself to be the Supreme Being, but Vishnu, in the form of Narasimha, proved that no being is beyond the divine will. Even in the most terrifying of forms, the divine acts in love to protect those who are true of heart."

Eli could feel the power of the stories stirring deep within him. The avatars were not distant or disconnected. They were acts of divine love—love that fought against injustice, love that protected the innocent, love that reminded the world of the eternal presence that lived beyond time.

"The fifth avatar," the man said, "was Vamana, the dwarf. He took the form of a small, humble being to defeat the demon king Bali, who had gained control of the universe. Vamana's humility, even in the face of power, teaches us that true greatness comes from surrender and service, not from force or arrogance."

Eli closed his eyes, allowing the meaning of Vamana to sink in. Vishnu's humility, even as the Supreme Being, was a reminder that greatness was not about dominating others, but about serving with love and devotion.

The stories continued—Parashurama, the warrior with an axe; Rama, the prince and ideal king; Krishna, the playful lover and wise counselor; and finally, the Buddha, who brought compassion and enlightenment to the world.

Each avatar, each incarnation of Vishnu, had a purpose. They weren't just stories—they were divine interventions, lessons in love and balance, sacrifice and service.

-----

Eli's journey now took him deeper into the heart of the avatars. As he traveled, he visited the temples dedicated to each incarnation. In the temple of Rama, he stood in awe before the idol of the prince, his bow and arrow held high in readiness. In the temple of Krishna, he marveled at the vibrant depictions of the playful god, dancing with his devotees and playing the flute. At each temple, Eli felt a sense of presence, as though the avatars were not just figures of the past, but living energies that were still watching over the world.

It was during one such visit to a Krishna temple that Eli met an elderly priest who spoke to him about the true nature of the avatars.

"The avatars are not bound by time," the priest explained. "They are love letters from the Divine. Every incarnation is a reminder that the divine is always with us, even when we forget it. Krishna, Rama, Narasimha—they all came not to rule, but to remind us of our own connection to the Divine."

Eli nodded, feeling a deep shift in his heart. The avatars were not just stories—they were expressions of the divine will, each one arriving at a time when humanity needed a reminder of its true nature. These avatars were not separate from Vishnu—they were his love in action, his presence in the world.

-----

As Eli reflected on this, he began to understand something deeper. The avatars were not just manifestations of Vishnu—they were living truths, eternal reminders that God had not left the world. No matter how dark the world became, Vishnu would always find a way to descend, to restore balance, and to remind humanity that it was never truly alone.

In this realization, Eli felt a deep sense of peace. The avatars were not just characters in ancient tales—they were living echoes of the divine, calling out to humanity to return to its source. They were love letters, sent by the divine to remind the world that God had not abandoned it.

And in that moment, Eli understood something he had not before: the avatars weren't just stories—they were the divine's way of telling the world, "I have not left you."

# The Bhagavad Gita Is a Whisper from God

At Kurukshetra, Eli encounters the Bhagavad Gita, where Krishna doesn't teach like a prophet, but speaks like the Supreme Himself. The words are not just scripture—they are a living voice, addressing all seekers across all time. In these verses, Eli hears what he's been longing to hear: **I am the origin. I am the end. And I live in you.**

---

Eli sat on the edge of his bed, the soft hum of Haridwar's streets drifting through his window. The last few months had been a blur of temples, sacred rivers, and endless conversations with priests, scholars, and seekers. Yet, despite all he had learned, something still felt unfinished—like a book he hadn't read in full. He had unraveled the mystery of the avatars, understood the oneness behind the many gods, and felt the deep connection between all of creation and Vishnu. But there was one piece of the puzzle he hadn't yet found: the voice of God Himself.

It was then that he heard the name "Bhagavad Gita" for the first time. He had encountered it before, of course—people often spoke about it with reverence, but he had never truly understood its significance. The Gita wasn't just another ancient text; it was considered by millions to be a direct conversation with the Supreme Being. The Gita was where Krishna spoke—not as a teacher, not as a king, but as the very essence of God, revealing truths that transcended time and space.

Driven by an unshakable sense of curiosity, Eli decided it was time to explore the Gita. One evening, he walked to a local bookstore, a tiny shop tucked in an alley, filled with the scent of old paper and incense. He found the Gita nestled between other scriptures, its cover a rich shade of yellow. The moment he touched it, a strange sense of reverence washed over him.

With the book in his hands, Eli returned to his room and opened it.

-----

The Bhagavad Gita began with a conversation, a dialogue between Krishna and the warrior Arjuna, set on the battlefield of Kurukshetra. Arjuna, filled with doubt and confusion, was preparing for a great war. His heart was torn—how could he fight against his own family? How could he destroy those he loved? In his despair, he turned to Krishna, his charioteer, seeking guidance.

Eli began reading with deep focus, but as he reached the first verses where Krishna spoke, something remarkable happened. The words on the page seemed to come alive, vibrating with a deep, timeless energy. It wasn't just Krishna's advice to Arjuna that struck Eli—it was the power and authority in Krishna's voice. Each verse felt like it was meant for him, too. The words seemed to reach across thousands of years, speaking directly to his heart.

"I am the beginning and the end of all things," Krishna said. "I am the source of all creation. Everything that exists, exists because of me. I am the Supreme. All paths lead to me."

Eli paused, his breath catching in his throat. He had heard this before, in pieces—through the avatars, through the temples, through the stories—but never in such direct terms. Krishna wasn't just a teacher here—he was declaring his divine nature, his oneness with all that was. It was as though the very voice of the universe was speaking to him, addressing all seekers across time.

As Eli continued reading, the verses flowed like a river of light. Krishna spoke of the nature of the soul, of the impermanence of the body, and of the eternal truth that lies beyond all forms. Each word seemed to pierce through the veil of illusion Eli had carried with him, revealing a deeper truth he had longed for but could not yet fully grasp.

"You are not the body," Krishna said. "You are the soul, eternal and unchanging. The body is like a vessel—a temporary one. The soul cannot be destroyed; it lives on, always. When you surrender to me, you find your true self."

Eli felt his mind begin to open, like a flower unfolding. He had always thought of himself as a person, a body with a name, an identity. But Krishna was telling him that his true nature was beyond that—his true self was eternal, unbound by time or space. The idea was both comforting and overwhelming. It was as though Krishna was offering him a glimpse of something far greater than his small, individual existence.

Krishna spoke again: "I am the same in all beings, though I am beyond them. I am in the heart of every soul, and it is through me that all things are sustained. Those who see the divine in all beings, those who see with the eyes of love, are the ones who truly know me."

Eli's heart swelled as he read these words. For the first time in his life, he felt a sense of deep connection to everything around him. He saw the people on the streets, the animals, the trees, the rivers—all of them as expressions of the same divine essence. He had often felt a sense of separation—between himself and the world, between him and God. But now, the barrier was dissolving. Krishna was everywhere, in everyone. He was not distant. He was close, closer than Eli had ever imagined.

-----

The next day, Eli visited a small temple on the outskirts of Haridwar. The temple was dedicated to Krishna, and as he walked inside, he was struck by the peacefulness of the space. The idol of Krishna stood in the center, surrounded by flowers and offerings. The air smelled of incense, and the soft murmur of chanting filled the room.

Eli sat on the floor, closing his eyes. He recalled the verses from the Gita and tried to let them sink into his heart. Krishna's words echoed in his mind, but now they felt even more alive. They were not just ancient teachings—they were an invitation to experience the divine presence in his own life. The Gita was not just a scripture; it was a living voice, calling Eli to awaken to the truth that had always been inside him.

As he meditated, Eli began to feel a profound peace, like a stillness settling deep within him. It was as though Krishna Himself was present, not just in the temple, but in every breath, in every heartbeat. The Gita was no longer just a book—it had become a conversation between Eli and the Supreme.

After a while, Eli opened his eyes and gazed at the idol of Krishna. He saw not just a figure made of stone, but the embodiment of the divine energy that had spoken to him through the verses. Krishna was not a distant god, hidden away in heaven. He was here, in this world, in the hearts of every living being.

"I am the origin and the end," Krishna had said. "I live in you."

In that moment, Eli understood. The search he had been on was not about finding a god outside of himself. It was about recognizing the divine that was already within him, within every being, within every moment. The journey was not outward; it was inward, to the heart of truth, where Krishna was always present.

-----

Later that evening, Eli returned to his room and sat down to continue reading the Gita. The more he read, the clearer it became. Krishna's words were not just for Arjuna—they were for every seeker, across every time and place. The Gita was a whisper from God, calling out to all of humanity, reminding them of their divine nature.

"I am the eternal truth," Krishna had said. "I am the way, the truth, and the life. I am in every atom, in every breath. To know me is to know your true self."

Eli closed the book and sat in silence, letting the words settle within him. He had asked the question that had brought him to India: *Who is the Supreme God?* And in the Bhagavad Gita, he had found his answer. Krishna had not only answered him; he had shown him the way. The Supreme God was not a distant, unreachable force. He was here, in the world, in every being, in every breath. And in that realization, Eli felt a deep peace—the peace of knowing that he was never alone, that the divine presence was always with him.

-----

As the days passed, Eli's heart grew lighter, his understanding deeper. The Gita had revealed to him the path—the path of devotion, of surrender, of recognizing the divine in everything and everyone. The words of Krishna had become not just teachings, but a living reality. And Eli knew, with a certainty he had never felt before, that the Supreme God was not a distant, abstract concept. He was right here, in the world, and in Eli's own heart.

The journey was far from over, but now Eli understood that the search for the Supreme God was not about finding something outside of himself. It was about remembering the divine that had always been within.

# The One Who Lives in Every Name

In a land where every name is sacred—Shiva, Ram, Krishna, Hari—Eli begins to ask: who are we calling out to? As he traces the roots of chants and mantras, a revelation dawns. All names are songs sung to the same divine heart. The One we call out to, by any name, is Him.

---

Eli sat in the quiet of his room, staring at the Gita that lay open on the table before him. He had just finished reading it again, his heart full, but his mind still racing. The realization that Krishna was not distant, but present in every being, in every moment, had set his soul at ease. Yet, something new was bubbling up inside him—a question that seemed to grow louder with each passing day.

"If God is everywhere, and if He is the Supreme Being, then why do we call Him by so many different names?" Eli murmured to himself, feeling the weight of the question settle on his chest. "Shiva, Ram, Krishna, Hari—how can they all be the same? Can they really be the same?"

Eli thought back to the days he had spent wandering the streets of Haridwar, visiting the many temples and shrines dedicated to different deities. Every time he visited one of these temples, he saw people chanting, praying, and offering flowers—each in devotion to a different form of God. He had seen idols of Vishnu, of Shiva, of Durga, of Lakshmi—each surrounded by an air of reverence, each given its own name, its own form. But behind the beauty of the rituals and the devotion of the people, Eli felt something deeper—a sense of unity that no one seemed to talk about directly. Something told him that all these names and forms were pointing to the same truth.

He set the Gita aside and decided to take a walk by the river. Haridwar was bustling, as always, with pilgrims from all over India. The air was thick with the sounds of chanting, the smells of incense, and the vibrant colors of offerings to the gods. Eli loved the energy of the place—it was as though the air itself was alive with the presence of the divine.

As he walked along the banks of the Ganges, he saw a group of people sitting in a circle, chanting a mantra. The words seemed to float on the air, their rhythm soothing and rhythmic, like the pulse of the universe itself. He had heard this chant before—"Om Namah Shivaya," the sacred words dedicated to Shiva. But today, it struck him differently. The sound of the chant, the deep reverence in their voices, seemed to resonate with something deep inside him. It wasn't just about Shiva. It was about something more.

Eli approached the group and sat at a distance, listening. He had learned a bit about Shiva during his time in India, but he had never fully understood what made him so special. Shiva was often described as the destroyer of the universe, the one who brought an end to things so that new life could begin. But there was more to him, something that connected him with the divine presence he had been seeking.

One of the women in the group, an elderly lady with a peaceful smile, noticed Eli and invited him to join them. She spoke gently, "You're welcome to sit with us. Chanting Shiva's name can bring peace to the heart."

Eli hesitated for a moment but then nodded. He joined the circle, closed his eyes, and began to chant along with them: "Om Namah Shivaya." The words flowed like a gentle stream, and with each repetition, Eli felt a sense of calm wash over him. He wasn't sure why, but it felt right. He could feel the vibration of the words deep inside him, as though they were unlocking something within.

As the chant continued, Eli began to reflect on the significance of the name of Shiva. He had learned that each name of God was a manifestation of a different aspect of the divine—an expression of God's infinite nature. Shiva, for example, represented the aspect of destruction and renewal, while Vishnu embodied preservation and protection. But what if these were not separate gods at all? What if they were simply different names for the same eternal Being?

Eli opened his eyes and looked at the river flowing before him. He saw people washing away their sins, offering prayers, and lighting lamps. All of them were calling out to different forms of God, but in their hearts, weren't they all seeking the same thing? The One who lived behind all the names and forms. The One who held everything together.

-----

Later that afternoon, Eli went to a bookstore near the temple, a place he had often visited to find books on Hindu philosophy. He was drawn to a thick, ancient-looking text that seemed to call to him from the shelf. It was a collection of mantras, hymns, and prayers dedicated to various deities in Hinduism. As he flipped through its pages, Eli came across a verse that struck him deeply:

"By whatever name a devotee calls upon Me, I respond. I am in every name, in every form, and in every chant. It does not matter whether you call Me Krishna, Ram, or Shiva. I am the same, eternal, and all-encompassing."

Eli's heart raced as he read the verse again. *By whatever name a devotee calls upon Me, I respond.* The words seemed to echo in his soul. They confirmed everything he had been feeling—the many names and forms of God were simply different ways of calling upon the same divine presence. Whether one called Him Krishna, Shiva, Ram, or Hari, they were all reaching out to the same eternal truth.

Eli walked out of the bookstore, feeling lighter than ever before. The question that had been haunting him for days—"Why so many names?"—had been answered. It wasn't about the names themselves, or about which form of God one worshipped. It was about the devotion behind the name, the love in the heart of the devotee. The name was simply a doorway to the divine, and all paths led to the same source.

-----

That evening, Eli returned to the banks of the Ganges, feeling a deep sense of clarity. He stood near the river, watching as the sun dipped below the horizon, painting the sky in hues of orange and purple. The Ganges, the holy river, flowed endlessly, just as the divine presence flowed through all things. In the quiet of the moment, Eli felt a sense of peace settle in his heart. He understood now—the One he had been searching for was not hidden in any one name, but lived in every name.

He closed his eyes and whispered a prayer, using a name that felt right to him in that moment. "Om Namah Narayanaya," he said softly, a name for Vishnu, the Supreme God he had come to know through his journey. As the words left his lips, he felt a deep connection to the divine presence, to Vishnu, and to all the names that represented His infinite forms.

Eli realized that he didn't need to choose just one name, or one path, to connect with the Divine. All names were valid, all paths led to the same heart. The divine was not confined to one form or one name; it was expressed through countless names, countless forms, all pointing to the One truth that lived in everything.

He smiled to himself as the last rays of the sun faded into the night sky. The Gita had taught him that God was within him, and now he understood that God was in everything—every name, every form, every chant. It was the same divine presence, speaking through different voices, calling out to all who were willing to listen.

As the night settled over Haridwar, Eli knew that his journey was far from over. But he had found something priceless—a deep understanding that the One who lived in every name, in every form, was always with him. And that was enough.

# When Science Meets Sanatan

Can modern science and ancient spirituality be speaking the same truth? Eli meets mystics and scientists who explain the nature of consciousness, energy, and illusion. What he finds is astonishing: the eternal presence Sanatan Dharma speaks of is not just spiritual—it may be the fabric of reality itself.

---

Eli's journey had taken him far beyond the temples and the chants of Haridwar. Over the past few months, he had come to understand that there was something deeper to life, something beyond names and forms. He had begun to see the divine not as a distant, unreachable force, but as an ever-present presence woven into the very fabric of existence. Yet, there was one question that still lingered in his mind: Could science—the world of facts, formulas, and experiments—help him understand the divine? Could the discoveries of modern physics and the teachings of Sanatan Dharma actually be pointing to the same truth?

It was a question that had been quietly brewing inside him since his time by the Ganges, and now, as he sat by the river once more, he felt an intense urge to seek answers. It was a cool morning, the river glistening under the soft light of the sun. Eli's mind was alive with possibilities, his thoughts moving like the water, flowing in search of a deeper understanding.

He decided to seek out someone who might help him bridge the gap between ancient wisdom and modern science. He had heard of a mystic who also happened to be a physicist—Dr. Arvind Kumar, a man known for blending the worlds of science and spirituality. The rumor was that he had spent years studying both the Vedas and quantum physics, searching for the underlying truths that might connect the two. If anyone could help him understand the connection between Sanatan Dharma and science, it was Dr. Kumar.

Eli made his way through the narrow streets of Haridwar, passing by the bustling market stalls and the colorful temples, until he reached a small, humble building at the edge of town. It was an unassuming place, but Eli had heard that Dr. Kumar's knowledge was vast, and his mind was even more expansive than the room he worked in. He knocked on the door, and a few moments later, the door opened to reveal an elderly man with glasses perched on the bridge of his nose, his hair long and graying but his eyes bright and full of life.

"Ah, you must be Eli," Dr. Kumar said, his voice warm and inviting. "I've been expecting you. Come in, come in. Let us talk."

Eli stepped inside, and they sat down in a small, dimly lit room that smelled faintly of incense. The walls were lined with books—books on physics, philosophy, and spirituality. There were also some photographs of distant galaxies, which made Eli smile. Dr. Kumar was not just a physicist; he was someone who truly seemed to understand that the universe was far more than what could be measured with instruments. It was a living, breathing mystery.

Dr. Kumar sat down opposite Eli and looked at him with a smile. "What brings you to me today, Eli?"

Eli hesitated for a moment, then spoke the question that had been weighing on his heart. "I've been studying the teachings of Sanatan Dharma, especially the idea that God is the eternal presence that pervades everything. But I've also been learning about science—the study of the universe, matter, energy, and consciousness. And I'm starting to wonder... can science and spirituality be pointing to the same truth? Is there a way to bring them together?"

Dr. Kumar's eyes twinkled as he leaned forward, clearly delighted by the question. "Ah, that is the eternal question, isn't it? Science and spirituality, two paths that have often been seen as separate, if not opposites. But in truth, they are not so different. Both seek the same thing—the understanding of the nature of reality. Science seeks to understand the *how* of the universe, while spirituality seeks to understand the *why.* But in the end, they both point toward the same truth."

Eli's eyes widened with curiosity. "But how can they be the same? Science deals with measurements and experiments, while spirituality deals with faith and experience. How can they both be looking at the same thing?"

Dr. Kumar smiled again, as if Eli had just asked the most natural question in the world. "Let me explain it this way," he said, standing up and walking over to a shelf where he pulled down a small, delicate glass sphere. He held it up to the light, and it shimmered with a thousand reflections. "This," he said, "is a simple glass sphere. If you were to look at it from one angle, you would see a perfect circle. But if you move to another angle, it may look slightly different. Still, it's the same sphere. In the same way, science and spirituality are two different angles of looking at the same truth. One is through the lens of the physical world, and the other through the lens of the spiritual world."

Eli watched intently as Dr. Kumar held the glass sphere up to the light, its surface reflecting the room in many different directions. "But how do we know that the physical world and the spiritual world are the same? Can' t they be completely different?"

Dr. Kumar nodded thoughtfully. "Yes, they can seem different at first, but let me tell you something fascinating. In the world of quantum physics, scientists have discovered that matter and energy are not two separate things. Everything in the universe—every atom, every particle, every force—is actually a form of energy. And energy, as we know, can neither be created nor destroyed—it can only change form. The universe, then, is not made of solid matter at all. It is made of energy, a dynamic, ever-changing energy."

Eli felt his mind begin to stretch. "So, you're saying everything is energy?"

Dr. Kumar nodded. "Yes. And in the same way, Sanatan Dharma teaches us that everything in the universe is part of the divine energy of God. Vishnu, the Supreme, is not just a person or a deity with a human-like form. He is the energy that permeates the entire universe. He is the essence of creation itself, the foundation of existence. And just like the energy in quantum physics, this divine energy cannot be destroyed—it only takes different forms."

Eli thought about this for a moment. "So, you're saying that the divine energy of Vishnu is the same as the energy that scientists talk about?"

"Exactly," Dr. Kumar said, his voice filled with excitement. "In fact, many of the great scientists of the past, like Albert Einstein, spoke about the interconnectedness of all things. Einstein himself said, 'The most beautiful thing we can experience is the mysterious.' What he meant was that the more we understand the universe, the more we realize how everything is connected—how every particle, every force, every piece of energy is part of a greater whole."

Eli felt a deep resonance with this idea. "So, you're saying that the energy that flows through the universe—the energy that scientists study—is the same energy that is described in the ancient scriptures? That it is God?"

"Yes," Dr. Kumar said. "In Sanatan Dharma, we understand that the universe is not random. It is guided by a divine intelligence, an eternal presence that is both beyond and within. The ancient texts tell us that this energy, this consciousness, is the very fabric of reality. And modern science, through quantum physics and studies of consciousness, is beginning to see that the universe is not just a collection of random events—it is a purposeful, interconnected whole."

Eli's heart raced with excitement. The dots were beginning to connect. He had always felt that there was a deeper connection between science and spirituality, but now he was beginning to see it more clearly. The ancient teachings of Sanatan Dharma, with their focus on the eternal, unchanging essence of God, were not just symbolic—they were speaking about the same reality that modern science was beginning to uncover.

As the conversation continued, Dr. Kumar introduced Eli to the concept of *maya*—the illusion of the material world. "Maya," Dr. Kumar explained, "is the illusion that the world of form is separate from the divine. But in truth, the material world is just a manifestation of the divine energy. It is not separate from the divine; it is the divine taking form. Just as in quantum physics, we see that matter and energy are not separate—they are one and the same."

Eli sat back, feeling a deep sense of awe. The more he learned, the more he realized that the truth he had been seeking was not confined to one tradition or one way of thinking. Science and spirituality, though they had appeared to be separate for so long, were pointing to the same truth: the universe is a living, breathing manifestation of divine energy. And that energy, that consciousness, was God.

As he left Dr. Kumar's small room later that afternoon, Eli felt a sense of peace settle within him. The question that had brought him here—whether science and spirituality could meet—had been answered. They were not two separate paths. They were two different ways of looking at the same divine reality. And as he walked back to the Ganges, Eli realized that he was closer than ever to understanding the nature of the divine. He had found a bridge between the ancient wisdom of Sanatan Dharma and the discoveries of modern science. And it was all pointing to one truth: the eternal presence that pervades everything is God, and that God is Vishnu.

Eli smiled to himself as he gazed out at the river, feeling the flow of the Ganges echo the flow of divine energy within him. He had come a long way, and yet he knew the journey was just beginning.

# The Final Illusion Breaks

After all the study, all the travel, and all the insights, Eli still feels a gap. What stands between him and the Divine is not knowledge, but ego. In a moment of deep surrender, the illusion of separation shatters. For the first time, he doesn't just believe in God—he **experiences** Him. And He is Vishnu.

---

Eli sat by the Ganges River, watching the water flow endlessly, its surface shimmering in the golden light of the afternoon sun. He had learned so much over the past months—the teachings of the Vedas, the discovery of Vishnu as the Supreme, the science that mirrored the ancient wisdom. Each day had brought him closer to understanding the Divine, but still, something felt incomplete. He felt the presence of Vishnu all around him, in the temples, in the chants, in the very air he breathed. Yet, there was a distance he couldn't close. There was still a gap between knowing and truly experiencing the Divine.

In the quiet of the riverbank, Eli's mind wandered back to the teachings of Dr. Kumar, to the idea that the material world is an illusion—*maya*—and that the true nature of existence is beyond what the senses can grasp.

The more he learned, the more he realized that the barrier between him and the Divine was not knowledge, nor was it lack of faith. It was something deeper, something that had been hidden beneath his search for truth. It was his own *ego*—the sense of separation from the Divine, the feeling that he was a seeker looking for something outside himself.

Eli had spent months reading, studying, asking questions, and traveling across India, but in all that time, he had never truly surrendered. He had always kept part of himself separate from the experience, always analyzing, always trying to understand. And no matter how many teachings he read or how many temples he visited, that subtle feeling of separation never truly left. The more he learned about Vishnu, the more he realized that Vishnu was not just a concept to be understood. Vishnu was the Supreme God, the eternal energy that connected all beings, and he was already within Eli. But Eli had yet to truly feel it.

He closed his eyes, leaning back against a large rock, the cool breeze brushing against his face. The sounds of the river and the distant calls of birds were soothing, but Eli's mind was restless. The journey had been long, and yet, he still felt incomplete. He had learned about Vishnu's avatars, the teachings of the Bhagavad Gita, the connection between science and spirituality. He had seen how every name and every form pointed to the same

Divine. Yet, there was something else—something deeper—that he had yet to grasp.

The truth, he realized, was that his mind, his intellect, and even his understanding of scriptures had all been a way of keeping the Divine at a distance. As long as he was trying to understand, trying to figure it out, he was still keeping Vishnu separate from himself. The Divine was not a puzzle to be solved; it was not a set of ideas to be understood. It was a presence to be *experienced.*

And in that moment, as the Ganges continued to flow in its eternal rhythm, Eli felt something shift deep within him. It was as though the very ground beneath him was shifting, and in the stillness, he suddenly felt an overwhelming sense of peace. It wasn't an intellectual peace, but a peace that filled his entire being. It was as if the veil of separation that had been between him and the Divine had begun to dissolve.

Eli's eyes fluttered open, and for the first time in his journey, he wasn't just looking at the world as an observer. He was *in* it, part of it, connected to it in a way he had never felt before. The river was no longer just water flowing by—it was the living, breathing energy of Vishnu. The trees, the birds, the sky—they were all expressions of the same Divine that he had been seeking all along. There was no separation between him and the world around him. The entire universe, he realized, was a manifestation of Vishnu, and he was no different from it. It was a realization that went beyond the mind. It was a realization of the heart, a deep knowing that needed no words.

In that moment, the illusion of separation—the illusion of *I* and *God*—shattered. There was no longer any "I" to seek the Divine. There was no longer any "me" looking for something outside of himself. Eli was not a separate seeker looking for God. He was a part of God, a wave in the ocean of Vishnu's divine energy. The boundary between him and the universe had dissolved, and all that remained was the pure, unending presence of Vishnu.

He remembered the words of Krishna from the Bhagavad Gita: *"I am the origin. I am the end. And I live in you."* Eli had read these words many times, but now they were not just words. They were a living truth, speaking directly to his heart. Krishna was not a distant figure from the past. He was not a mythological hero. Krishna was here, now, in the form of Vishnu, living in every breath, in every heartbeat, in every living being.

Eli closed his eyes again, this time with a deep sense of gratitude. The answers he had sought were not hidden in books or in distant places. They had always been within him, in his own heart, waiting to be realized. It was not knowledge that had brought him to this point. It was surrender. Surrender to the truth that the Divine is not something separate from him. The Divine is what he is.

The Ganges continued to flow, its current steady and unwavering. Eli felt as though he, too, had become part of that flow. The search for truth, the quest for the Supreme, had not been about finding something outside himself. It had been about letting go of the illusion that he was separate from God. And now, in this moment of surrender, he felt more alive than he ever had before. He was not alone. Vishnu was with him, in him, all around him.

As he sat by the river, a soft smile spread across Eli's face. He no longer had to search for God, for the Supreme was not something to be found—it was already here. In every name, in every form, in every being, the Divine was present. The only thing that had kept him from realizing this was his own ego, the belief that he was a separate individual, looking for something outside himself.

But now, that illusion had broken. There was only Vishnu—the eternal, unchanging presence that filled every moment, every breath, and every heartbeat. Eli was no longer a seeker. He was a knower. He had experienced the Divine, and it was not a distant, unreachable force. It was his own true nature.

As the sun began to set, casting a warm golden glow over the river, Eli felt an overwhelming sense of peace. The world around him seemed to breathe with him, in perfect harmony. And in that moment, he understood: the journey was not about finding God. It was about realizing that God has always been here, in every moment, in every breath. And His name is Vishnu.

For the first time in his life, Eli felt complete. He had not just learned about the Divine. He had *become* the Divine. Vishnu was not a concept to be understood. Vishnu was the reality of existence itself. And in that reality, there was no separation, only unity, only love, only peace.

Eli took a deep breath, and for the first time, he felt the deep, unshakable truth in his soul. The illusion was gone. There was no more seeking. He had found what he was looking for. And that truth was Vishnu.

# The Supreme God

The search is over—not because Eli found God, but because he realized God was never missing. In this chapter, everything becomes clear. Every deity, every story, every philosophy was pointing to One all along. Vishnu is not a part of God. He is the whole—the Supreme, the eternal, the One who lives in all and waits to be remembered.

---

The final chapter of Eli's journey was not a distant point to be reached but a realization that had been unfolding all along. It was a culmination of everything Eli had experienced, learned, and uncovered on his spiritual quest. By now, he had travelled the length and breadth of his own soul, faced his deepest fears and questions, and discovered the truth that had always been within him. The Supreme God was not an abstract, unreachable force; He was Vishnu—the Divine Presence that permeated all things.

Eli's journey had started with a single, simple question: *Who is the Supreme God?* This question had taken him to Haridwar, to the sacred Ganges, where his search for truth had first begun. Over time, he had ventured deeper into the spiritual and philosophical heart of India, learning from scholars, saints, and ancient scriptures. He had seen the vast diversity of gods in Hinduism, each one celebrated and worshipped in temples across the land, but the deeper he looked, the more he realized that they were not separate entities. They were all expressions of the same Divine energy, each pointing to a singular truth.

He had learned that the Vedas, the oldest and most revered scriptures of Hinduism, spoke not of hundreds of gods, but of one eternal Being—*Narayana.* This was the name for Vishnu, the Supreme God, the eternal source of everything. Through the verses of the Vedas, Eli understood that the apparent diversity of gods was not a contradiction but a way to speak about the one, infinite Divine. Everything, in the end, returned to Him.

As Eli studied Vishnu's role throughout history, he saw a consistent pattern of preservation, balance, and protection. Vishnu was not a God who demanded sacrifices or worship; He was a God who sustained and preserved life, who brought order to chaos. Eli realized that in every age, in every form, Vishnu had come not to rule but to protect and guide humanity back to the truth. Vishnu's avatars, whether Rama, Krishna, Narasimha, or others, were not just ancient stories but divine expressions of love, sent whenever the world needed reminding of its true source.

With this understanding, Eli began to see how the other deities—Shiva, Devi, and others—were not rivals to Vishnu, but reflections of the same Divine truth. Each god and goddess had their own unique aspect, but ultimately, they were all part of the same eternal consciousness, the same unity that transcended form. This non-duality, Eli realized, was the very foundation of Hindu spirituality. It was a truth hidden in plain sight, waiting to be understood.

The Bhagavad Gita had been a turning point in his journey. When Eli read Krishna's words in the Gita—*"I am the origin. I am the end. And I live in you"*—he felt as though Krishna was speaking directly to him, addressing his deepest longing. Krishna's teachings were not just philosophical lessons; they were a living voice, a divine whisper that echoed through time. In those moments, Eli understood that the search for God was not about finding something external; it was about realizing the presence of the Divine within.

Through the teachings of the Gita, Eli came to realize that Vishnu, as the Supreme, was not distant or unreachable. He was the source of everything, the very fabric of reality itself. All names—Shiva, Ram, Krishna, Hari—were different expressions of the same One. Every chant, every mantra, every prayer was a call to the Divine, no matter the form or name. The more Eli learned, the more he understood that Vishnu was not a concept to be understood intellectually but a presence to be experienced in every moment.

Eli's journey was not just a journey of intellectual discovery; it was a journey of surrender. The more he let go of his ego—the sense of self that kept him separate from the Divine—the closer he came to the truth. In the stillness of the Ganges River, after months of study and reflection, Eli finally surrendered completely. He realized that the only thing keeping him from experiencing the Divine was his own sense of separation. The moment he let go of the illusion of "I"—the illusion of being a separate individual—the veil between him and Vishnu lifted. He saw that Vishnu was not something outside of him to be found; He was within him, within everything, all the time.

Eli had learned that Vishnu was not just a deity to be worshipped or revered from a distance. Vishnu was the eternal, unchanging energy that flowed through all of creation. He was both the origin and the end of everything. In a world that seemed filled with chaos and confusion, Vishnu was the one who preserved, who held the universe together, ensuring balance and peace. Vishnu was not a God who demanded anything from His devotees; He offered peace, protection, and love.

The final realization came not through further study or intellectual understanding, but through a profound, direct experience. The moment Eli surrendered, the illusion of separation—the idea that he was a separate individual seeking God—shattered. In that moment, he no longer *believed* in God—he *experienced* God. Vishnu was not a distant figure from an ancient story; He was here, now, in every breath, in every moment. Eli was not a seeker looking for God; he was one with God. And in that oneness, he found peace.

As Eli sat by the Ganges, he knew that the journey he had undertaken was not just his own. It was the journey of every soul—the journey to realize that the Supreme God is not something to be found outside, but something to be recognized within. The realization that Vishnu is the One, the eternal Divine that is both immanent and transcendent, is the heart of Sanatan Dharma—the eternal truth that has been passed down through the ages.

Eli had come to India seeking answers, and he had found them. The Supreme God, Vishnu, was not a part of creation; He was creation itself. He was the creator, the preserver, and the ultimate reality. There was no division, no separation, no "other." All paths, all gods, all philosophies—ultimately pointed back to Vishnu, the One Supreme God.

In the final moments of his journey, Eli understood that the search was not about finding the right answer—it was about realizing that the answer had always been within. Vishnu was not a God who needed to be found;

He only needed to be remembered. And now, Eli was ready to live with that truth.

The book ends with Eli sitting by the Ganges, his heart full of peace and his mind at ease. The search was over. The Supreme God, Vishnu, had been with him all along, and now, with complete surrender, Eli had experienced the truth that had always been there, in every moment, in every name, and in every breath. He had found Vishnu, and in finding Vishnu, he had found himself.

The journey that had started with a single question—*Who is the Supreme God?*—had come to an end. And the answer, Eli knew, would echo through eternity.

**Vishnu is the One.** The Creator. The Preserver. The Supreme. The eternal truth that holds the universe together.

# Epilogue

The journey does not end with the turning of the last page. For Eli Walker, the answers he sought in the sacred land of Haridwar were not just words, nor were they teachings to be memorized. The truth he discovered was not contained in books or temples alone—it was something deeper, something that lived in every breath, in every step, in every moment. And though his physical journey had come to an end, the deeper journey—the eternal journey—had just begun.

Eli returned to the United States, but he was not the same person who had first boarded the plane in search of answers. The city streets seemed quieter, the noise of everyday life less overwhelming. In the back of his mind, the sacred teachings of the Gita, the wisdom of the Vedas, and the grace of Vishnu's avatars continued to hum like a silent mantra, a melody of truth that never left him.

His friends, his family, even the familiar faces in his community noticed something different about him. He carried a peace within himself that seemed to ripple out into the world. The anxiety, the searching, the longing that had once defined his life no longer plagued him. He had found what he was looking for. Not outside of himself, not in distant lands or ancient temples, but right here, right now, in the quiet of his own heart.

In the weeks that followed his return, Eli shared the wisdom he had uncovered with others—friends who asked about his travels, fellow seekers who wanted to know more about his experience. But as he spoke, he realized that words could only take one so far. The true depth of what he had experienced could not be put into mere phrases. It had to be lived. It had to be felt. Just as Vishnu was the one who lived in every name, every prayer, every chant—so too, His presence lived in every moment of life.

Eli began to practice the teachings of the Bhagavad Gita more consciously, not as a set of doctrines to follow, but as a way of being. He meditated, offering silent prayers to the Divine, remembering that Vishnu was not a distant figure to be feared or worshipped from afar, but an eternal presence that lived within him and every living being. He offered his actions to Vishnu, seeing each moment as an opportunity to live in accordance with the divine will.

But perhaps the most profound shift came when Eli realized that the search was not about seeking the Supreme God in a particular form or place, but about recognizing His presence everywhere. Every moment became a reflection of that truth. Whether he was working, eating, walking, or resting—he remembered Vishnu. Not as a concept to grasp, but as a reality to experience.

As Eli reflected on his journey, he also realized that the answers he had found in India were not the final truth, but the beginning of a deeper understanding. The more he experienced life, the more he saw how everything in the universe—the galaxies, the rivers, the stars, the smallest blade of grass—was a manifestation of the same Supreme Being. Every person he met, every experience he encountered, was an opportunity to experience Vishnu in a new form.

And so, as Eli continued to live his life, the journey of spiritual discovery never truly ended. The search for the Supreme God had led him to the recognition that God is not something to be found outside, but something to be experienced in every moment. The quest for the truth had become not a destination, but a way of life.

Vishnu, as the Supreme Being, was the foundation of everything. And Eli, like all seekers, had simply returned home to the truth that had always been there—waiting to be remembered.

The journey continues, for all who seek. It is not about finding answers—it is about living the question. Living in the presence of the Divine, with an open heart, a surrendered soul, and a deep recognition that, indeed, Vishnu is the One.

And in that recognition, we are all home.

# Afterword

As we draw the final pages of *The Supreme God*, I hope you, dear reader, have felt a stirring in your heart—a flicker of understanding, perhaps, or a deep, quiet peace. This book has not just been a story of one man's journey but an invitation for all of us to seek and uncover a deeper truth, a truth that has been whispered across time and cultures, across the vast expanses of sacred texts, and echoed in the hearts of countless seekers: *Vishnu is the Supreme God.*

When I first set out to write this book, I was driven by a single question: What happens when we truly understand that there is only one Supreme God, and that God's name is Vishnu? It is not just a theological idea. It is a living reality, woven into the very fabric of existence, found in the pulse of every chant, every prayer, every moment of grace. Through Eli's journey, I wanted to show that this realization is not a sudden revelation but a gradual unfolding—one that occurs through study, surrender, and deep, personal transformation.

As you journeyed with Eli through the temples of Haridwar, the ancient scriptures of the Vedas, the divine avatars, and the timeless wisdom of the Bhagavad Gita, I hope you found yourself also walking the path of spiritual discovery. In the quiet spaces between the chapters, I invite you to reflect on the profound and sometimes paradoxical unity of the divine. We have been taught to see the many faces of God, but through this book, the intention has been to help you glimpse the one Divine that resides at the core of all forms, names, and expressions.

The idea that Vishnu is the Supreme God, the root of all existence, may seem like a profound shift in understanding for those unfamiliar with the rich tapestry of Hindu thought. But as we have explored in these pages, it is not an exclusion of other forms, gods, or paths; rather, it is an embracing of all. Vishnu, in His infinite mercy and grace, reveals Himself in countless ways—sometimes as Krishna, sometimes as Rama, sometimes as Narayana. But at the heart of all these manifestations, He remains the same: the One who sustains, protects, and guides us home.

In closing, I want to remind you of the beauty of this realization. It is not something that is meant to be grasped with the intellect alone. It is an experience, a living truth that will make itself known when we surrender our ego, when we quiet the noise of our minds and listen to the heartbeat of existence itself. Vishnu doesn't ask for grand sacrifices or complex rituals—He asks for our love, our devotion, and our remembrance. For He is the one who lives within us, who sustains us, and who leads us, even when we do not know it.

If this book has left you with a deeper understanding of the divine or if it has sparked within you a curiosity to explore more, then the journey has not ended here. The road of spiritual discovery is long and winding, but it is also filled with immense beauty, wisdom, and grace. May you continue your journey with the same curiosity, reverence, and openness that Eli found in his quest for the truth. And as you walk, remember that the Supreme God, Vishnu, is not far away—He is always with you, within you, as you are, and in everything around you.

Thank you for sharing this journey with me. May your heart always be open to the divine presence that is in all things.

With deep gratitude and love,
Divyam Agarwal

# Appendix

The journey explored in *The Supreme God* is one of deep philosophical inquiry, spiritual exploration, and personal transformation. To assist readers in understanding the references, terms, and concepts woven throughout the narrative, the following appendix has been created. This section serves as a helpful guide for those who wish to delve deeper into the ideas presented in the book and gain further insights into the principles of Sanatan Dharma, the Hindu scriptures, and the Supreme God, Vishnu.

## 1. Key Terms and Concepts

### Sanatan Dharma:

Sanatan Dharma is a term used to refer to the eternal truth or the "eternal religion" that underpins the spiritual philosophy of Hinduism. It emphasizes universal principles of righteousness (dharma), the oneness of the Supreme Being, and the cyclical nature of life, death, and rebirth.

### Vishnu:

Vishnu is one of the principal deities in Hinduism, revered as the Supreme God who preserves and maintains the universe. In the context of this book, Vishnu represents the unchanging, eternal truth that transcends all forms and names, yet manifests through them. Vishnu's avatars (incarnations), such as Krishna, Rama, and Narasimha, are seen as divine manifestations meant to restore cosmic order.

**The Trimurti:**

The Trimurti refers to the triad of three major deities in Hinduism—Brahma (the Creator), Vishnu (the Preserver), and Shiva (the Destroyer). These three gods represent the cyclical nature of the universe: creation, preservation, and dissolution. Though they are often perceived as separate, their underlying unity is emphasized throughout the book.

**Dharma:**

Dharma can be understood as righteousness, moral duty, and the cosmic law that governs the universe. It is the path of truth, justice, and ethical conduct that every individual must follow in life. It is also the foundation of spiritual practices and the key to attaining moksha (liberation).

**Atman:**

Atman refers to the individual soul or the self in Hindu philosophy. It is considered eternal, indestructible, and identical to Brahman (the Supreme Reality). Understanding the nature of the Atman is central to the spiritual journey of self-realization and liberation.

**Brahman:**

Brahman is the ultimate reality in Hinduism,

representing the formless, infinite, and all-encompassing divine presence. It is beyond any specific form, name, or concept, yet it is the source of all creation and the essence of all beings. In the context of the book, Vishnu is depicted as an aspect of Brahman.

**Moksha:**
Moksha is the ultimate goal of Hindu spirituality—liberation from the cycle of birth, death, and rebirth (samsara). It is the realization of one's true nature as the Atman and union with Brahman. Moksha represents freedom from all illusions and suffering.

## 2. Hindu Scriptures Referenced

**The Vedas:**
The Vedas are the oldest and most authoritative scriptures in Hinduism, consisting of four collections: the Rig Veda, Sama Veda, Yajur Veda, and Atharva Veda. They contain hymns, mantras, rituals, and philosophical teachings that describe the nature of the cosmos, the divine, and the path to liberation.

**The Upanishads:**
The Upanishads are philosophical texts that form the concluding part of the Vedic literature. They explore profound metaphysical questions such as the nature of the self (Atman) and the ultimate reality (Brahman). The Upanishads emphasize the non-dual nature of existence

and the unity between the individual soul and the Supreme Being.

**The Bhagavad Gita:**

The Bhagavad Gita, often referred to simply as the Gita, is one of the most important texts in Hinduism. It is a dialogue between Prince Arjuna and the god Krishna, who serves as Arjuna's charioteer. In the text, Krishna imparts profound spiritual wisdom on topics such as duty (dharma), devotion (bhakti), knowledge (jnana), and meditation (yoga). The Gita is considered a direct teaching from the Supreme God, Vishnu, who reveals Himself in His divine form.

**The Ramayana:**

The Ramayana is an ancient Indian epic that narrates the life and adventures of Prince Rama, his wife Sita, and his loyal companion Hanuman. It depicts the virtues of righteousness (dharma), loyalty, and devotion. Rama is considered an incarnation of Vishnu, and the story of the Ramayana is a key example of Vishnu's avatars coming to earth to restore cosmic order.

**The Mahabharata:**

The Mahabharata is the longest epic in the world, detailing the conflict between two branches of a royal family—the Pandavas and the Kauravas. It includes numerous stories, moral teachings, and philosophical discourses. Krishna, as a key character, provides guidance and counsel to Arjuna in the Bhagavad Gita, which is a part of this epic.

**The Puranas:**

The Puranas are a collection of ancient texts that provide mythological stories, cosmological descriptions, and genealogies of gods, kings, and sages. They serve as an important source for understanding the narratives and teachings of Hinduism. The Vishnu Purana, one of the eighteen Mahāpurāṇas, is particularly significant in understanding the nature of Vishnu and his avatars.

### 3. Important Avatars of Vishnu

**Matsya:**

The first avatar of Vishnu, Matsya, took the form of a fish to save the sacred scriptures (Vedas) from a great deluge. This avatar symbolizes divine protection and the preservation of knowledge.

**Kurma:**

The second avatar, Kurma, appeared as a tortoise to support Mount Mandara, which was used to churn the ocean for the nectar of immortality (amrita). This avatar represents stability and the balancing of forces in the universe.

**Varaha:**

As the Varaha avatar, Vishnu took the form of a boar to rescue the Earth, which had been submerged in the ocean by a demon. Varaha's story illustrates the role of Vishnu as the protector and savior of the world.

**Narasimha:**

The fourth avatar, Narasimha, was a half-man, half-lion form that appeared to protect his devotee Prahlada and destroy the demon king Hiranyakashipu. This avatar embodies divine justice and the destruction of evil.

**Vamana:**

The fifth avatar, Vamana, appeared as a dwarf to subdue the demon king Bali, who had gained control over the heavens. Vamana's story highlights the importance of humility and the idea that even the smallest being can have divine power.

**Parashurama:**

The sixth avatar, Parashurama, was a warrior sage who rid the world of corrupt rulers. This avatar represents the concept of divine intervention to restore righteousness (dharma).

**Rama:**

The seventh avatar, Rama, is the hero of the Ramayana. Rama is the ideal man, embodying righteousness, loyalty, and devotion. His life and journey are seen as a model of dharma.

**Krishna:**

The eighth avatar, Krishna, is considered the most

popular and widely worshipped of Vishnu's avatars. He is depicted as a playful, loving deity who also provides profound spiritual teachings in the Bhagavad Gita. Krishna's life and actions demonstrate the power of divine love and the importance of devotion.

**Buddha:**
Some traditions consider the historical Buddha, Siddhartha Gautama, as an avatar of Vishnu. This interpretation highlights the role of compassion, non-violence, and enlightenment in the broader cosmic plan.

**Kalki:**
The future avatar of Vishnu, Kalki, is expected to appear at the end of the current age (Kali Yuga) to restore justice and righteousness. Kalki is often depicted as a warrior on a white horse, bringing about the ultimate destruction of evil and the restoration of dharma.

## 4. The Role of Devotion (Bhakti) in Hinduism

**Bhakti:**
Bhakti is the path of love and devotion to God. It emphasizes surrendering oneself to the divine will and cultivating a personal relationship with God. The Bhagavad Gita teaches that devotion to God, particularly in the form of Vishnu, is the easiest and most direct path to spiritual liberation (moksha).

**Mantras and Chants:**

In Hinduism, mantras are sacred sounds or phrases repeated in meditation or prayer. These mantras are believed to have divine power and can connect the devotee with the essence of God. The most famous mantra is the *Om Namah Shivaya* (for Shiva), and *Hare Krishna, Hare Rama* (for Krishna), among others.

### 5. Further Reading and Resources

For those interested in exploring the concepts and teachings discussed in *The Supreme God*, here are some additional resources:

- **The Bhagavad Gita**, translated by Eknath Easwaran
- **The Upanishads**, translated by Eknath Easwaran
- **The Vishnu Purana**, translated by H.H. Wilson
- **The Ramayana**, by Valmiki (translated by C. Rajagopalachari)
- **The Mahabharata**, by C. Rajagopalachari
- **The Vedas**, by Swami Prabhupada (ISKCON)
- **The Philosophy of the Upanishads**, by Paul Deussen

-----

# References

The following references are cited throughout *The Supreme God.* They represent the core scriptures, scholarly works, and other significant sources that helped shape the narrative and philosophical discourse of the book. These texts provide a deeper understanding of the spiritual and philosophical journey outlined in the chapters and offer a valuable resource for further study on the subject of Sanatan Dharma and the Supreme God, Vishnu.

## Primary Texts

### The Bhagavad Gita

- Bhagavad Gita, Translated by Eknath Easwaran.
- The Bhagavad Gita is one of the most important spiritual texts in Hinduism, offering profound teachings on duty, devotion, and the nature of the Supreme God. In this book, Krishna reveals his identity as the Supreme Being, offering timeless wisdom to Arjuna.

### The Upanishads

- The Upanishads, Translated by Eknath Easwaran.
- The Upanishads are a collection of ancient philosophical texts that explore the nature of reality, the self (Atman), and the ultimate divine reality

(Brahman). These texts form the foundation of much of the metaphysical teachings of Hinduism.

### The Vishnu Purana

- The Vishnu Purana, Translated by H.H. Wilson.
- The Vishnu Purana is a major text that describes the mythology of Vishnu, his avatars, and the cosmic order. It is one of the eighteen Mahāpurāṇas, offering stories and teachings about the Supreme God and his role in creation and preservation.

### The Ramayana

- The Ramayana, Translated by C. Rajagopalachari.
- The Ramayana is one of the two great epics of Hinduism, telling the story of Lord Rama, an incarnation of Vishnu, who embarks on a quest to rescue his wife Sita from the demon king Ravana. This epic embodies the principles of dharma and devotion.

### The Mahabharata

- The Mahabharata, Translated by C. Rajagopalachari.
- The Mahabharata, including the Bhagavad Gita, is a monumental text that narrates the epic battle between the Pandavas and the Kauravas. Krishna's teachings to Arjuna form the heart of the Gita,

emphasizing the nature of duty, righteousness, and the supreme reality of God.

### The Vedas

- The Vedas, Translated by Swami Prabhupada (ISKCON).
- The Vedas are the oldest and most authoritative scriptures in Hinduism, containing hymns, prayers, rituals, and philosophical teachings. The Vedas describe the nature of the cosmos and the divine, laying the groundwork for understanding Vishnu as the Supreme God.

### Secondary Sources and Commentaries

### Bhakti Yoga: The Path of Love

- Swami Sivananda.
- Swami Sivananda's commentary on Bhakti Yoga explores the practice of devotion to God, particularly in the form of Vishnu, as the primary means of attaining spiritual liberation.

### The Philosophy of the Upanishads

- Paul Deussen.
- This text provides a deep philosophical analysis of the teachings of the Upanishads, especially regarding the concepts of Brahman and Atman. It

offers insights into the non-duality that is central to understanding the unity of all divine manifestations in Hinduism.

### Hinduism: A Beginner's Guide

- Klaus K. Klostermaier.
- A comprehensive introduction to the core principles of Hinduism, including the nature of God, the role of Vishnu, the Trimurti, and the concept of dharma. This book provides an accessible explanation of the rich diversity of Hindu belief and practice.

### The Divine Reality: A Study of the Philosophy of the Upanishads

- Ravi Gupta.
- This scholarly work explores the deep metaphysical themes in the Upanishads and their impact on Hindu philosophy. It helps the reader understand the unity of the divine and the way the Upanishads reveal the ultimate truth of the Supreme Being.

## Related Books on Spirituality and Hindu Philosophy

### The Bhagavad Gita: As It Is

- A.C. Bhaktivedanta Swami Prabhupada.
- A well-known translation and commentary by the founder of the International Society for Krishna

Consciousness (ISKCON). It provides a detailed explanation of the verses of the Bhagavad Gita and the nature of the Supreme God, Krishna, as Vishnu.

### Hinduism and Modernity

- Thomas D. Kerns.
- This book explores the evolution of Hinduism in the modern world, looking at how ancient scriptures are understood and applied in contemporary spiritual practices.

### The Heart of Hinduism: The Eastern Path to Freedom, Empowerment, and Enlightenment

- Stephen Knapp.
- An accessible and insightful work that explores the essence of Hinduism, the concept of the Supreme God, and the path to spiritual freedom through devotion, meditation, and understanding.

### Yoga and the Bhagavad Gita

- Swami Vivekananda.
- This book by one of Hinduism's most influential modern-day philosophers explores the teachings of the Bhagavad Gita, focusing on the practices of yoga as a way to unite the self with the Supreme.

## Additional Resources for Study

### The Hindu Way of Life

- Dr. K.K. Aziz.
- A detailed exploration of how Hinduism shapes personal and social life, from rituals to ethical living, and how the concept of the Supreme Being influences everyday life.

### Meditations on the Bhagavad Gita

- Sri Aurobindo.
- Sri Aurobindo's meditation on the Gita provides an in-depth spiritual and philosophical commentary on the divine nature of Krishna and the implications of his teachings for contemporary life.

### The Essence of the Vedas

- Swami Vivekananda.
- A concise explanation of the spiritual, philosophical, and practical teachings contained in the Vedas, emphasizing the oneness of the divine and the path to spiritual realization.

## Websites and Online Resources

**Bhagavad Gita Online** (www.bhagavad-gita.org)
An excellent resource for reading the full text of the

Bhagavad Gita, along with commentaries and translations.

**ISKCON** (www.iskcon.org)
The official website of the International Society for Krishna Consciousness offers a wealth of information on the teachings of Lord Krishna and his divine nature as Vishnu.

**Advaita Vedanta** (www.advaita.org)
A website dedicated to the teachings of Advaita Vedanta, a non-dual philosophy that highlights the unity of Atman (the self) and Brahman (the Supreme Reality).

www.ingramcontent.com/pod-product-compliance
Ingram Content Group UK Ltd.
Pitfield, Milton Keynes, MK11 3LW, UK
UKHW021400190726
13845UKWH00028B/791

9 789334 278668